INDIA
Land, Life and Culture

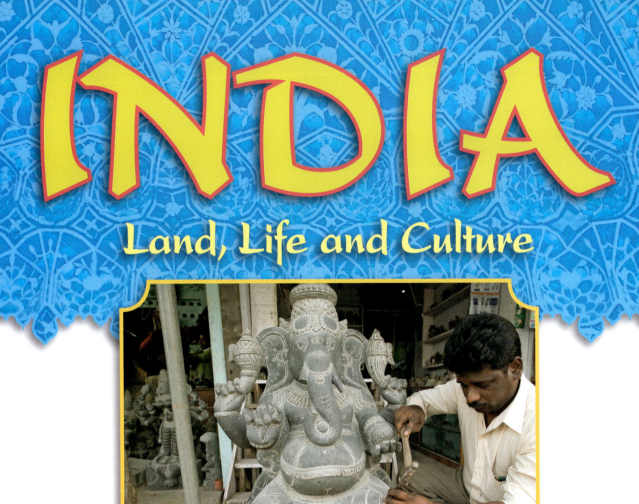

Arts and Culture

ROSEMARY SACHDEV

MACMILLAN LIBRARY

First published in 2009 by
MACMILLAN EDUCATION AUSTRALIA PTY LTD
15–19 Claremont Street, South Yarra 3141

Visit our website at www.macmillan.com.au or go directly to www.macmillanlibrary.com.au

Associated companies and representatives throughout the world.

Copyright © Rosemary Sachdev 2009

All rights reserved.
Except under the conditions described in the *Copyright Act 1968* of Australia and subsequent amendments, no part of this publication may be reproduced, stored in a retrieval system, or transmitted in any form or by any means, electronic, mechanical, photocopying, recording or otherwise, without the prior written permission of the copyright owner.

Educational institutions copying any part of this book for educational purposes under the Act must be covered by a Copyright Agency Limited (CAL) licence for educational institutions and must have given a remuneration notice to CAL. Licence restrictions must be adhered to. Any copies must be photocopies only, and they must not be hired out or sold. For details of the CAL licence contact: Copyright Agency Limited, Level 15, 233 Castlereagh Street, Sydney, NSW 2000. Telephone: (02) 9394 7600. Facsimile: (02) 9394 7601. Email: info@copyright.com.au

National Library of Australia Cataloguing-in-Publication data

Author: Sachdev, Rosemary.
　Arts and culture / Rosemary Sachdev.

　ISBN 978 1 4202 6714 3
　Sachdev, Rosemary. India: Land, life and culture.
　Includes index.
　For primary school age.
　Arts – India – Juvenile literature. India – Civilization – Juvenile literature.
　India – Social life and customs – Juvenile literature.

954

Edited by Kath Kovac
Text and cover design by Peter Shaw
Page layout by Kerri Wilson
Photo research by Lesya Bryndzia
Illustrations by Damein Demaj, DEMAP

Printed in China

Acknowledgements
Dedicated to Jasbir, who gave me India, and to Arkin, Amaya and Naira who belong and who will read these books some day.

With special thanks to the Archaeological Survey of India in New Delhi and Aurangabad for permission to take photographs in the Ajanta Caves with a camera and tripod, and thanks to the National Museum of India, Janpath, New Delhi for permission to photograph replicas in the Museum shop. Lastly, many thanks to La Boutique, Sunder Nagar, New Delhi, for the photograph of their joint family and their help in allowing us to photograph prints, paintings and artefacts from their collection.

With many thanks to all those who gave time for photographs and interviews, for lending their children to be photographed and for helping in the many ways they did and especial thanks to Jatinder, without whose tireless travel and wonderful photographs, these books would never have happened.

All photographs courtesy of Jatinder Marwaha except for:
DreamPictures/Getty Images, **17** (bottom); La Boutique, New Delhi, **11** (top, middle); National Museum Shop, **5** (top); Photolibrary/Alamy/Hornbil Images, **20** (top); Collection of RJ Sachdev, **5** (bottom); RJ Sachdev, **20** (bottom); Beata Pastuszek/iStockphoto, **16**.

While every care has been taken to trace and acknowledge copyright, the publisher tenders their apologies for any accidental infringement where copyright has proved untraceable. Where the attempt has been unsuccessful, the publisher welcomes information that would redress the situation.

Contents

India, a land of diversity	4
An ancient culture	5
Festivals	6
Painting	10
Sculpture	12
Tribal and folk art	14
House decoration	15
Music	16
Dance	18
Theatre	20
Film	22
Literature	24
Textiles	26
Jewellery	28
Arts and culture today	30
Glossary	31
Index	32

Showing respect
Indian people always use titles with people's names to be polite, such as Shri and Shrimati if speaking Hindi, the national language, or Mr and Mrs if speaking English. These titles are different all over India, and their form depends on the family relationship or the seniority of the person addressed.

Glossary Words
When a word is printed in **bold**, you can look up its meaning in the Glossary on page 31.

India, a land of diversity

India is a land of great **diversity**, which can be seen in its arts, culture, people, landscape and climates. For every description of Indian life, there are many different but equally true variations.

India has a very long history. People have lived in India for around 10 000 years and come from many different racial backgrounds. They speak hundreds of languages; some spoken by millions of Indians, others spoken by only a few thousand. The country has many different landscapes and climates, from freezing mountains to hot, tropical areas.

India came under British influence in the 1600s, and Britain took control of India in the 1850s. India gained its independence from Britain in 1947 and became a **republic** in 1950.

Ancient carvings

Mountainous landscapes

Majestic tombs

Many religions

Unique plants

Wild animals

This book looks at India's art and culture. It explores traditions of literature, sculpture, music and dance that date back thousands of years, as well as the arts and culture popular today, such as the films of Bollywood and traditional crafts.

An ancient culture

India's ancient history is reflected in its art and culture. Indian people and the many waves of migration into India from nearby areas have added to India's rich cultural heritage for thousands of years. The oldest **artefacts** found in India were made by people from the ancient Indus Valley Civilisation (3500–1800 BCE). Many of these pieces, including sculptures, seals, pottery and children's toys, can now be seen in museums.

India's religious heritage is also evident in its culture. Many religious arts and festivals are found across India, where followers of all the world's religions live.

The 'Priest King' statue, from 2500 BCE, may be a portrait of a ruler from the Indus Valley Civilisation.

Did You Know?

The game of chess was invented in India. It was later adopted by the Persians and the Arabs.

For Your Information

Tribal people still live in India's forests and practise traditional crafts.

Madhubani folk art paintings are traditionally made by women from the district of Madhubani, in Bihar.

Festivals

India has many cultural and religious festivals. Somewhere, in some part of the country, there may be a festival being held almost every day of the year.

Each festival may have one or more different stories to explain the reason it is celebrated. Some people enjoy religious festivals simply for the fun and the special food, without necessarily belonging to that religion.

Holi

One of the most colourful festivals is Holi. It is celebrated mostly in northern India at the beginning of spring. People celebrating Holi have a lot of fun smearing each other with coloured powder or spraying coloured water on everyone. They sing and dance to the beat of drums and, at lunch time, stop to enjoy a special meal.

During Holi, which is also called the Festival of Colours, children have the freedom to smear colour on adults.

Did You Know?

Some Hindus also celebrate Holi by burning bonfires the night before the throwing of coloured powder, in memory of the burning of Holika, the daughter of a wicked king who sacrificed herself to save her brother.

People buy coloured powder in the markets to celebrate the Holi festival.

Dussehra

The festival of Dussehra symbolises the triumph of good over evil. Dussehra is celebrated by burning **effigies** of the ten-headed demon king Ravana, as well as his brother and son. Tall effigies are erected in parks and filled with fireworks. At sunset, the effigies are set alight.

Divali

Divali is one of India's most popular festivals. People remember the day that Ram brought his wife, Sita, back to his home city of Ayodhya. The people of Ayodhya lit lamps called diyas to welcome Ram and Sita home. To celebrate Divali, people buy new clothes, jewellery, kitchen utensils and sweets. As night falls, all the lights are left on, diyas or candles are lit outside houses, and fireworks are let off.

For Your Information

The story behind Dussehra is of Ram, a king's son, and Ravana, the demon king of Lanka. Ravana kidnapped Ram's wife, Sita. Ram fought with Ravana, defeated his army with the help of the monkey god, Hanuman, and rescued Sita.

Did You Know?

Diyas are clay lamps filled with oil or wax, and have a cloth wick.

The Divali festival is also called the Festival of Light, as children light fireworks.

Crowds cheer as effigies of Ravana and his brother and son are burned.

Id-ul-Futr

Id-ul-Futr is India's main Muslim festival. It is held after Ramzan, more widely-known as Ramadan, a time when Muslims do not eat or drink anything from sunrise to sunset for 40 days. During Ramzan, people remember the time that the prophet Mohammad spent alone in the desert, praying and fasting. Once the moon is sighted, Id-ul-Futr begins. On this day, everybody wears new clothes, goes to the mosque to pray, and then has a special festive meal.

Did You Know?

The Koran, the holy book of the Muslims, is said to have come to Mohammad after his time of praying and fasting.

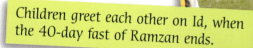

Children greet each other on Id, when the 40-day fast of Ramzan ends.

Even some non-Christian families have started celebrating Christmas, and place decorated Christmas trees in their homes.

Christmas

Christmas is celebrated all over India, even though the number of Christians living here is relatively small. At Christmas, Christians celebrate the birth of Christ. It is a time to have a festive meal with family and friends. Catholics go to midnight mass and Protestants go to Christmas services in churches decorated with coloured lights. Markets are also lit up with colourful lights and streamers and sell Christmas trees and decorations.

Rakhi

Rakhi celebrates the devotion of brothers and sisters.

Sisters tie coloured threads called a rakhi on their brothers' wrists. Brothers give their sisters a present and promise that they will always look after them.

For Your Information

Traditional Indian families were very large. All brothers would live together with their wives and children, their parents, and other relatives who had no sons. This was called a joint family. Cousins are still considered brothers and sisters, even if they do not live in a joint family.

Onam

The Onam festival is celebrated in Kerala when the **monsoon** season has ended and the growing season begins. The most famous feature of Onam is a boat race held in the backwater lagoons. Women decorate the floors of houses with patterns called rangoli.

Colourful and festive rangoli patterns are traditionally made using rice powder and vegetable colours.

MEET Saraswati Srimant Jagtap

Saraswati Srimant Jagtap lives near Pune. She learned to do rangoli at the age of 15. She decorates the courtyard of her house and her work place for ceremonies.

In conversation with Saraswati Srimant Jagtap

I don't decide the design beforehand. It flows from my mind and hand naturally. Some simple patterns I can do in about 15 minutes. This art is only done by women, never by men.

Painting

Indian paintings have been traced back more than 2000 years. Early styles of painting include prehistoric cave paintings, wall paintings and small pictures called miniatures on paper or ivory. Modern paintings may be on canvas, just as they are anywhere in the world.

Did You Know?
Some Indian paintings were done on dried palm leaves, tied together with string and placed between wooden boards to form books.

Ajanta Cave paintings

For Your Information

The subjects of many of the Ajanta Cave paintings are the Jataka tales, which tell stories of previous lives of the Buddha. These stories are very popular with children. Many of the later paintings show scenes from daily life. Visitors can see the king's court and how people dressed 1500 years ago.

The wall paintings in the Ajanta Caves were done by Buddhist artists to show the life of the Buddha. Some of these paintings are more than 2000 years old. The paintings were forgotten until 1819, when an English officer of the Madras Army stumbled across 27 caves in the jungle. The caves, which were carved out of living rock, contain paintings and sculptures and are now a **world heritage site.**

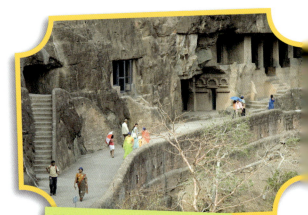
The Ajanta caves, seen here from the outside, are a popular tourist destination.

Ajanta cave paintings

To protect the colour of the paintings, they can no longer be seen in strong light. Flash photography is completely prohibited, but long exposures using a tripod can be taken with special permission. Guides are allowed to use special lights for very short periods of time. For most of the time, the caves are in dim light.

Miniature paintings

Miniature paintings are about 15 centimetres by 10 centimetres in size. They have been painted in India from about 1500 CE in the courts of Hindu and **Mughal** kings.

Hindu miniature paintings usually show the world of the Hindu gods and goddesses, or of court life of the kings. They often include writing as part of the painting's design. Mughal miniatures show portraits of kings, usually either surrounded by family and followers, greeting foreign travellers, hunting or listening to music. Other miniatures show animals and birds in great detail.

Modern Indian miniature paintings, such as this one depicting the god Krishna and his court, are still created using traditional methods.

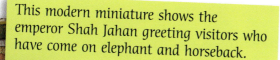

This modern miniature shows the emperor Shah Jahan greeting visitors who have come on elephant and horseback.

Modern painting

Many Indian artists have become well-known throughout the world. They mainly paint in non-traditional styles.

Some of India's famous painters include F.N. Souza, Anjolie Ela Menon, Tyeb Mehta, Satish Gujral and M.F. Hussain. Hussain was once a barefoot movie billboard painter and is still painting at more than 90 years of age.

MEET Paramjit Singh

Paramjit Singh joined the College of Art in Delhi in 1953. He became a lecturer at Jamia Millia University, where he could paint and teach, but left in 1992 to paint full time. He paints large landscapes. His wife and daughter are also artists, and the whole family exhibits their work worldwide.

In conversation with Paramjit Singh

As students we were taken to a forest of thorny trees and these have inspired me ever since. Mind and heart and hand must work together.

Sculpture

The oldest known Indian sculpture is of a small, bronze dancing girl. It is about 4500 years old and comes from the Indus Valley Civilisation. Human **torsos** in stone or **terracotta** have been found, as well as terracotta toys of birds and animals. Today, these are all in museums.

Most traditional Indian sculpture is religious. Many statues are of Hindu gods and goddesses, who can take either human or animal form.

The dancing Shiva

One of the most famous sculptured forms is of the god Shiva, performing a dance of destruction in a ring of fire. Dancing Shiva sculptures are usually made of bronze or other metals. The figure is nearly always represented in the same way, but it varies in size from about 15 centimetres to two metres across.

This dancing Shiva sculpture is from Tamil Nadu.

For Your Information

The god Shiva is one of the three gods who form a **trinity**. The three gods are:
- Brahma, the Creator
- Vishnu, the Preserver
- Shiva, the Destroyer.

Many old Hindu temples are covered with sculptures of individual human or animal figures.

Ganesha

Ganesha is the most popular Hindu god. He has the body of a man and the head of an elephant. Ganesha is a guardian and protector, and is in charge of good fortune, wisdom and learning. Even some non-Hindu Indians may have statues of Ganesha in their homes.

The figure of Ganesha is often modelled in clay, carved in stone or wood, moulded on terracotta plaques or carved on walls above doors.

Did You Know?

The most common explanation of why Ganesha has the head of an elephant is that his father, Shiva, mistakenly cut off his son's head in anger and replaced it with an elephant's head.

MEET R. Kothandan

R. Kothandan is a sculptor who lives in Mamallapuram. He studied to college level before deciding to follow sculpture. He has been sculpting for 15 years.

In conversation with R. Kothandan

I enjoy my work, it gives me pleasure. I work with the black Cuddapah stone, which is good for sculpting. The Ganesha I am working on will sell for 35 000 rupees but I won't sell one very often. On a typical day I get five buyers, mostly tourists, who want small images.

This stone Ganesha, also known as Ganapati, is being carved in Mamallapuram by sculptor R. Kothandan.

Tribal and folk art

The tribal people of India mostly live in the forests. They each have their own art forms. Different tribal areas of India are known for their clay or metal figures.

Terracotta and metal figures

Large, modelled terracotta horses are made in Bankura, in Bengal. They can be up to two metres high. Terracotta elephants, horses, camels and other animals are made in other areas of India.

Many tribal people make small iron or brass figures. These are often very long, thin, stylised figures of people or animals. Some people make them for the city markets.

The fragile tail and ears of these small Bankura horses are made separately, and later fitted to the figure in holes left for this purpose.

For Your Information

The Indian state of Orissa represents their gods in a particular style. The three gods can be made from clay, papier-mâché, wood or stone, but they always look the same.

Tribal metal sculptures

Brass elephants made in the Bastar district of Chhattisgarh may be small or large.

This brass figure of a woman wearing glasses and reading a book was made in Bastar for a city market.

This horse with riders is an example of the very thin, long figures made by some people of the Kutia Kond tribe who live on the Orissa–Andhra Pradesh border.

House decoration

The walls of many houses in Indian villages are often painted. The paintings may be of animals or people, painted in natural styles such as seen in the Rajasthan town of Shekawat or painted in stylised forms.

Wall painting

In Worli, near Mumbai, the brown plastered walls of houses are painted with white stick figures. The figures are small and may be arranged in circles or lines. The arrangement of the figures is part of the decoration.

In Shekawat, the walls of bigger houses were painted with scenes from daily life. This style became popular in the 1800s and early 1900s. The paintings were of Indian men in traditional costumes, riding elephants or horses, and Indian women, alone or flying kites with friends. In the 1900s, figures of British men in top hats and formal clothes riding in cars were also painted.

Modern-day Worli paintings may be painted on brown paper instead of house walls.

For Your Information

Worli paintings on paper are designed for the city markets and are not always done by the Worli people, but by artists who like the style and wish to use the original designs.

This wall painting on a house in Rajasthan depicts wealthy people riding in procession on horses, an elephant and a camel.

Music

There are many traditional Indian musical instruments. The tabla, dagga, hudkka and mridangam are types of drums. The shenai is similar to an oboe, and the bansuri is a flute. Stringed instruments include the sitar, the sarod, the tamboora and the veena. Singing is also an important form of Indian music.

For Your Information

The audience at an Indian concert will call 'wah, wah' when they think the music is very good. If the musicians do not hear this sound, they will think the audience is not enjoying the music.

Stringed instruments

Most stringed instruments have large **bulbous** ends and long necks. The strings are plucked. Indian musicians know the melody and the rhythm of what they need to play from memory. There is no written music, so the musicians **improvise** around a given discipline.

Drums

Different forms of drums are used in performances to supply the rhythm. The tabla and dagga, the most common drums used in concerts, look similar but are of slightly different sizes. They are both played at the same time. The mridangam and the hudkka are double-ended drums used in processions.

Did You Know?

Indian musicians sit on the floor when they perform.

A sitar is a stringed instrument with a large bulbous end.

Traditional vocal music

Indian traditional **vocal** music has two main styles. Hindustani music is from the north of India and Carnatic music is from the south. The singing is mainly devotional, with singers praising the gods.

The singer in this classical concert is playing the sitar, while the other musicians are playing the drums and the harmonium.

Gazal singing

The Gazal style of singing has been popular ever since the time of the Mughal courts, more than 400 years ago. The singer is accompanied by musicians playing drums and the harmonium, an instrument with a keyboard and a squeeze box. The songs were originally religious, but after being adopted by the Mughals, they are now about love of people or nature. Gazal evenings may be held in a private house or in a concert hall.

Songs in film

The most popular music in India comes from films. Many Indian movies are made in the Hindustani language in Mumbai and in the Tamil language in Chennai. Many Indians listen to songs from films on the radio, on television and on mobile phones.

This colourful song and dance scene is from a Hindustani film.

Dance

There are many forms of classical dance in India for both men and women. These dances generally depict scenes from the Hindu **epics.** Like Indian singing, many dances are semi-devotional, telling stories of the gods.

Dances for women

Many classical dance forms come from south India. A single dancer wearing ornate clothing and jewellery is accompanied by musicians sitting on one side of the stage. The dances incorporate hand, foot, head and eye movements. Every movement of the dance has its own meaning.

MEET Jeena Johnson

Teenager Jeena Johnson is a classical dancer who lives in Ernakulam, in Kerala.

In conversation with Jeena Johnson

I have been studying classical dance for five years now. I practice for an hour every day of the week and for three hours on Saturday and Sunday, as well as finishing my homework. I love dancing and my parents support me and want me to do as much as I wish. I would like to grow up to be a well-known classical dancer and show this art all over the world.

Traditional Indian dances

Bharatnatyam, a form of dance from Tamil Nadu.

Kuchipudi, a form of dance from Andhra Pradesh.

Mohiniattam, a form of dance from Kerala.

These teenage girls are learning classical dance at a dance school. Other classical dance forms are Odissi from Orissa and Manipuri from Manipur.

Dance for men

Kathakali, from Kerala, is a spectacular dance form. This dance is performed only by men, who also perform any women's parts. The men wear amazing masks and costumes. A new mask, painted on the performer using makeup, is worn for every performance.

This dancer is made up and ready for a Kathakali dance drama performance.

Kathakali dancers wear elaborate costumes.

Kathak dancers wear an ornate dress over trousers and have anklets of many bells that add to the music.

Kathak dance

The Kathak dance form developed in the Mughal court of the north. Kathak, which can be very active, is traditionally danced by women.

For Your Information

Modern dance forms are usually based on traditional forms, but without the rigid discipline. They may be danced by men or women or groups of dancers.

Folk dances

The Punjabi Bhangra folk dance is performed at times of celebration. When a groom arrives for his wedding procession, all his friends and relatives, men and women, will dance a form of Bhangra. Drummers in the procession provide the beat for the dancing.

The Gujarati Garba folk dance is also performed at celebrations. Women clap their hands while dancing in a circle. Folk instruments such as the drum keep the rhythm.

Theatre

The oldest form of Indian theatre is called the Ramlila. It is a series of plays based on the epic story of the *Ramayana*, which tells of the abduction of Sita, the wife of Rama, by Ravana, demon king of Lanka. The story continues with a fight to rescue Sita with the help of the monkey god, Hanuman, and the happy return of the couple to their home town of Ayodhya in the north of India.

Did You Know? The Ramayana features in all forms of art and culture in India.

The Ramlila

A small cast may perform the Ramlila in a theatre or on street corners. The Ramlila may also be performed at open **maidans** with a large cast of actors. The stories of these plays are well-known to all Indians.

Huge crowds enjoy the Ramlila, especially at the time of the Dussehra festival, which celebrates Ram's victory over Ravana.

Folk theatre

Puppets, especially shadow puppets, are popular in small Indian towns and villages. The puppet masters travel from place to place, putting on plays to entertain the local people in the evenings. The puppets are held behind a white, backlit screen.

Puppet performances in Rajasthan take place in front of a very large backdrop painted with hundreds of figures taken from the epics, such as the *Ramayana*.

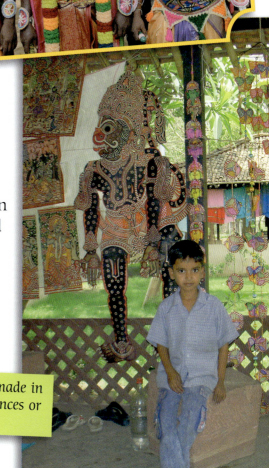

Brightly coloured leather puppets are made in large sizes if made for village performances or in small sizes if made for sale.

Modern theatre

Modern theatre is also popular in India. It is mainly shown in the bigger cities, where small theatres have been built especially for these performances. Plays are staged in many regional languages in the main cities, but regional-language theatre is more popular in the states where the language is spoken.

One of Mumbai's famous acting families is the Kapoors. Four generations of the family have starred in Indian films. About 30 years ago, the Kapoors decided they also wanted to act in live theatre and so they started the Prithvi theatre in Mumbai, named after the first Kapoor actor, Prithvi Raj Kapoor.

For Your Information

The Prithvi theatre in Mumbai stages plays in English, Hindi and Gujarati languages. The theatre compound is very lively and is a popular meeting place for young theatre people. Discussion groups hold meetings and children's plays are also staged in the school holidays.

The Prithvi theatre, in the Juhu area of Mumbai, is run by the Kapoor family.

Film

India has the largest film industry in the world. It is much bigger than the Hollywood film industry. Films from India are exported around the world and are becoming increasingly popular. Movie themes include family dramas and action/police/gangster plots. The plots are usually simple, but with many twists. The films are full of singing and dancing, and can run for three hours.

Did You Know?

Most Hindi films are made in Mumbai, which was formerly called Bombay, so the Mumbai film world has come to be known as Bollywood.

Bollywood produces about 1000 films a year, which are watched by over three billion people.

Films in the Hindustani language

Bollywood films have helped to spread the popularity of the Hindi language throughout India by using the commonly spoken form of Hindi, sometimes called Hindustani. People who speak different languages learn Hindi by watching the films.

Films in the Tamil and Kannada languages

The film industry in the southern languages, mainly Tamil and Kannada, is also large. Some of the stars of these films are so popular that they have gone on to become important politicians in India. Many people vote for them in elections, as the star's screen image is taken as true. One main Tamil actor, M.G. Ramachandran, became Chief Minister of Tamil Nadu.

This film was made in the southern language of Kannada.

Serious films

Serious films are also produced in India. Many serious Indian films have won awards and popularity throughout the world. However, they will never be as popular in India as Bollywood films. Although they share similar themes with Bollywood films, serious films are shorter in length and do not usually have any singing or dancing in them. Some Indian actors appear in both styles of film.

For Your Information

The first internationally known Indian film was called 'Pather Panchali' by the director Satyajit Ray. This film won many international awards in the 1950s.

MEET Vijay Krishna Acharya

Vijay Krishna Acharya is a Bollywood film writer–director. He has written many popular Hindi films and has just finished directing his first full-length feature film, *Tashan*.

In conversation with Vijay Krishna Acharya

I work in mainstream cinema because I can tell a story to many people in India and the world. People see a lot of films in a year and get pleasure from them. People not only need escape from mundane realities but need entertainment. It's not a luxury but the essence of the modern man who needs to eat, sleep and be entertained!

Vijay Krishna Acharya hard at work on his latest creation.

Literature

Literature has always been a part of Indian culture. The stories of the *Mahabharata* and the *Ramayana* have been well-known for around 3000 years, but were not written down until about 1600 years ago.

The Mahabharata

The *Mahabharata* tells the story of two rival related families **vying** for the throne. The heroes are the five sons of King Pandava. A great battle between the two families is described in detail in this piece of literature.

For Your Information

There is no actual proof that the stories of the *Mahabharata* are real history. However, Sonipat and Panipat, the towns that the families are meant to have come from, still exist just north of Delhi. Remains of buildings from 2300 years ago have been found in Indraprastha, in south Delhi.

A section of the *Mahabharata*, called the Bhagavad Gita, was turned into a moral book that advised Hindus on how they should live their lives.

The story of the *Ramayana* has been depicted in books, theatre, dance, film and television serials.

The Ramayana

The Ramayana tells the story of Sita, Ram's wife, who was kidnapped by the evil king of Lanka. The story is well-known throughout India and it is also known in South-East Asia. Carved panels depicting scenes from the story are on temples in Thailand, Cambodia and Indonesia.

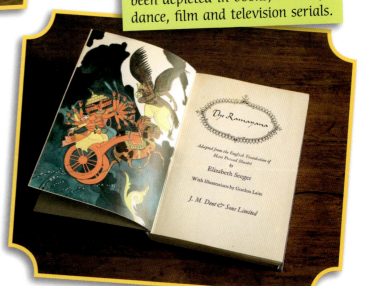

Literature in many languages

All parts of India have a strong literary tradition. Many books are published in all the regional languages as well as Hindi. A large group of Indians also write in English. Four of these authors, Salman Rushdie, Arundhati Roy, Kiran Desai and Aravind Adiga, have won the **Booker Prize** for literature over the last 30 years.

Religious books

There are many books related to Hinduism in India. The *Vedas* are a series of books about Indian philosophy written about 3000 years ago. The *Vedas*, the *Mahabharata* and the *Ramayana* were all written in Sanskrit, the classical language of India that is still used by Hindu priests.

Children's books are written and translated into all the regional languages of India, and published by the National Book Trust of India.

Did You Know?

The Mughal emperors were very fond of having their life histories recorded. Lots of information about their lives from their arrival in India in 1526 onwards is available.

These Booker Prize-winning books are by Kiran Desai (*The Inheritance of Loss*, 2006), Salman Rushdie (*Midnight's Children*, 1981), Arundati Roy (*The God of Small Things*, 1997) and Aravind Adiga (*The White Tiger*, 2008).

Textiles

Indian people have grown, spun and woven cotton textiles and silk for thousands of years. Most Indians wear cotton clothes that are draped around them, as the climate is mainly hot. In northern India, winters are cold, so silk can be worn comfortably. Women in the warmer south of India will wear silk all year, as so much silk is woven in the south.

Saris and shawls

Silk saris are worn by women throughout India. Saris are usually 5.5 metres long, but can be around eight metres long in some areas. When the weather is cold, Indian men and women wear woollen shawls. The best shawls are spun and woven in Kashmir.

Men's woollen shawls are usually plain, but women's shawls are often skilfully embroidered.

MEET Nissar Ahmed

Nissar Ahmed is a shawl weaver from Kashmir. He has been weaving shawls for 10 years.

In conversation with Nissar Ahmed

I want my children to study and better their lives, I'd like my daughter to be a doctor and my son to be a teacher.

Nissar Ahmed takes 10 days to weave a plain shawl and about six months to weave a shawl with a complex pattern.

Carpets, durries and numdahs

The designs of handmade woollen carpets, which are traditionally red, were originally influenced by Persian carpets. Durries are woven cotton or woollen floor coverings that are plain, striped or have geometrical designs. They are much cheaper than carpets, so are used by more people. Numdahs are small rugs from Kashmir, made from felt and embroidered with floral or animal patterns.

Folk embroidery

Many of India's desert and tribal women make elaborately embroidered clothing for themselves. The embroidery uses cotton thread and small mirrors, shells or coins.

Carpets and folk embroidery

Phulkari embroidery from Punjab uses satin stitch to cover large surfaces, such as bed or cushion covers.

This handknotted carpet from Kashmir has a central design in one direction and can be used as a prayer rug.

This traditional red carpet from Kashmir has a central design and geometric border.

This tribal woman wears a very elaborate embroidered blouse and head covering.

Jewellery

Indians are very fond of jewellery, as both ornaments and a sign of wealth. In the past, before the days of banks, jewellery was used as a safe method of keeping family wealth. If the rains failed and crops did not grow, the family could always sell some gold jewellery to survive until the following harvest.

Did You Know?
Brides in India do not traditionally wear wedding rings. Instead, they are given at least two gold bangles to show they are married.

Gold jewellery

All Indian women wear some type of gold jewellery every day. Little girls are often given gold at birth, and will usually have their ears pierced before their first birthday. Little gold studs will be placed in her ears to keep the holes open. Brides are given at least two sets of gold jewellery, one by her family and the other by her husband's family. Men are less attached to jewellery as day wear, but many wear rings and a chain, and some wear ear studs.

The gold used in Indian jewellery is 22 **carat**. This is much softer than the 14- or 18-carat gold usually worn in western countries, and is worth more money.

Each set of wedding jewellery will usually have a necklace, earrings, bangles, a ring and often a hair piece.

Some of India's gold jewellery is set with precious stones, rubies, emeralds or sapphires and worn for celebrations and parties.

Silver jewellery

In many regions of India, especially the desert regions of Rajasthan and parts of Gujarat, heavy silver jewellery is worn instead of gold. Women in these areas wear silver necklaces, earrings, bangles and rings, as well as very heavy ankle bracelets and toe rings.

Camel bone jewellery

Some tribal women of Rajasthan wear many bangles all the way up both arms. They used to wear ivory bangles, but ivory, which comes from elephant tusks, is now banned, so they wear camel bone bangles instead.

Silver jewellery is popular in some areas of India.

Precious stones and enamelled jewellery

Kundan jewellery is encrusted with precious stones. Meenakshi jewellery, inspired by Mughal jewellery, is **enamelled** in different colours on a gold backing. Navratna rings and pendants have nine different precious stones set in gold.

For Your Information

Necklaces of semi-precious stones such as coral, turquoise, garnet and topaz are often sold to tourists. Indians rarely wear these stones, unless they are set in gold or silver.

These Kundan jewellery earrings may have Kundan work on the front and Meenakshi work on the back.

Arts and culture today

The Indian government supports all aspects of Indian arts. Art academies promote traditional arts as well as encouraging talent in modern forms of art. The government also supports craftspeople, as do many private organisations.

Craft villages

In craft villages, craftspeople can come and work, as well as sell their crafts. All states have their own craft emporiums, selling their special state crafts and designs.

Cottage industries

A number of specialised government-run shops, known as Cottage Industries Emporiums, source high quality handicrafts throughout India.

Khadi shops sell the hand-spun, hand-woven cloth that was made popular by Mahatma Gandhi, the unofficial leader of the movement for independence from Britain.

Did You Know?

Every state has its own special crafts, which they sell at handicraft shops in their states and in the major cities.

The Dilli Haat craft fair in Delhi usually has a special theme, which changes every two weeks, featuring a particular region or a special type of craft.

Craftspeople can sell their goods on stalls at the Dilli Haat craft fair for a maximum of two weeks a year.

Glossary

artefacts	objects made by people that have become of historical interest
Booker Prize	an annual prize for the best original novel in English written by a citizen of a Commonwealth country
bulbous	bulb-shaped
carat	measurement of the purity of gold or the weight of diamonds or gems
diversity	great variety
effigies	three-dimensional likenesses of people
enamelled	colour applied and fired in a number of layers
epics	long poems, originally recited, telling the stories of heroes
improvise	perform original music without previous preparation
maidans	open spaces in a village, town or city used for community activities
monsoon	seasonal wind bringing heavy rain
Mughal	Muslim rulers of India from the 1500s to the 1800s
republic	a form of government where the rulers are elected by the people and the leader is usually called the President
terracotta	brownish red clay, often used in pottery or tiles
torsos	upper bodies
trinity	a group of three closely connected things or people
vocal	sound produced by a voice
vying	competing
world heritage site	a place decided by UNESCO as being of outstanding value to the world

Index

A
Ajanta Cave paintings 11
art 10, 11, 14, 15

B
Bollywood 22, 23
Booker Prize 25
Buddha 10

C
carpets 27
cave paintings 10
chess 5
Christmas 8
cotton 26
craft 5, 30

D
dance 18, 19
Divali 7
drums 16, 17
Dussehra 7

E
embroidery 27

F
festivals 6, 7, 8, 9
film 17, 22, 23
film songs 17
folk art 14
folk theatre 20

G
Ganesha 13

H
Hindi 21, 22
Hindu 11, 12, 13, 24
Hindustani 17, 22
house decoration 15

I
Id-ul-Futr 8
Indus Valley Civilisation 5

J
jewellery 7, 28, 29
joint family 9

K
Kannada language 22
Kashmir 26, 27

L
literature 24, 25

M
masks 19
miniature paintings 11
modern theatre 21
Mughal 11, 17, 19, 25, 29
Mumbai 15, 17, 21, 22
music 16, 17
musical instruments 16

O
Onam 9

P
painting 10, 11, 15
precious stones 28, 29
puppets 20

R
Rahki 9
rugs 27

S
Sanskrit 25
saris 26
sculpture 12, 13
semi-precious stones 29
shawls 26
Shiva 12
silk 26
singing 16, 17

T
Tamil language 17, 22
terracotta 14
textiles 26, 27
theatre 20, 21
tribal art 14

V
vocal music 17